This is the true story of Yasha,
a little moon bear cub.

Saving Yasha
The Incredible True Story of an Adopted Moon Bear

By Lia Kvatum

Photographs by National Geographic Young Explorer
Liya Pokrovskaya

NATIONAL GEOGRAPHIC
WASHINGTON, D.C.

In early spring, when the snow was still deep, in a den inside a big hollow tree, Yasha was born. There, he and his mother lived, warm and snug. But one day, hunters came and Yasha's mother was gone.

Rough hands grabbed Yasha. Creatures with two legs instead of four put him in a box with bars so he couldn't escape. There were many smells he had never experienced. He cried because he could not feel his mother's warm fur.

But soon more two-legged animals arrived. Yasha knew by now that these were people. Yasha shrank back in fear. But these were two gentle scientists named Liya and Sergey. They silently offered Yasha a bottle full of milk, and gazed quietly at him as he guzzled it down. It tasted very good.

Yasha felt better, and he wanted more. He followed Liya and Sergey deep into the forest.

Nestled in leaves, beneath brown, crooked oaks and pointy pines sat a small wooden house. Liya and Sergey had built it especially for orphaned bear cubs. Yasha was very curious about the new house and everything around it.

He sniffed and explored inside and out.

Yasha was happy with his new home. A few days later, two other orphaned cubs named Shum (rhymes with gum) and Shiksha (SHIK-sha) came to live in the house. They pawed and clawed at each other. Yasha hid behind Liya's legs, while the little black cubs stared at him, surprised. Slowly, the three cubs sniffed one another. Before too long, they were all rolling, biting, and playing.

Together the cubs and the scientists became a family.

Right away, Yasha and his new family explored their woodland home. Liya ran through the forest. The cubs shuffled along after her.

By the time they were four months old, Yasha, Shum, and Shiksha practiced climbing up and down trees every day—up, up, up, and upside down until they were exhausted.

Yasha explored and snuffled at holes in tree trunks . . .

. . . and at flowers on the ground.

He nibbled lots of green plants and learned which ones he liked best.

As Yasha learned how to live in the woods, Liya and Sergey watched him. Yasha would shuffle over, touching Liya softly, wanting her to play. But Liya was a person, not a bear. So she stayed still and silent.

The scientists were always kind and gentle, but they wore special clothing to cover their smell and never talked or played with the cubs. They wanted to make sure the cubs would grow up to live as wild bears.

Seasons passed and soon snow would cover everything like a thick, white blanket. The moon bear cubs had fluffy coats and were fat from munching the nuts and fruits of the forest. Yasha grew very sleepy. Liya and Sergey built their cubs a den and gave them colorful ear tags to wear to keep them safe from hunters.

Yasha crept into his warm den and closed his eyes. He slept . . . and slept . . . and slept . . . for almost six months.

The snow melted. The wild bear in Yasha knew it was time to wake up. He grew even stronger this year and was beginning to understand how to survive on his own, venturing farther and farther into the Russian wilderness.

One summer day when Yasha was playing deep in the forest he heard a ROAR! Yasha's heart jumped in his chest. But he knew just what to do! He ran as fast as he could and scrambled up a tree. When he was high above the ground he looked down . . .

IT WAS A TIGER! The tiger jumped at him, raking its claws down the brittle bark, snarling and roaring. But Yasha had escaped, and eventually the tiger moved on. Yasha sat there, scared and crying, until Shum and Shiksha climbed up to be near him.

Yasha was happy to see his family and proud that he had escaped one of the most dangerous predators in the forest.

Yasha was now ready to become truly wild. The scientists were happy. The bears were safe to roam free under the sun and sleep snug under the moon.

Yasha's Home

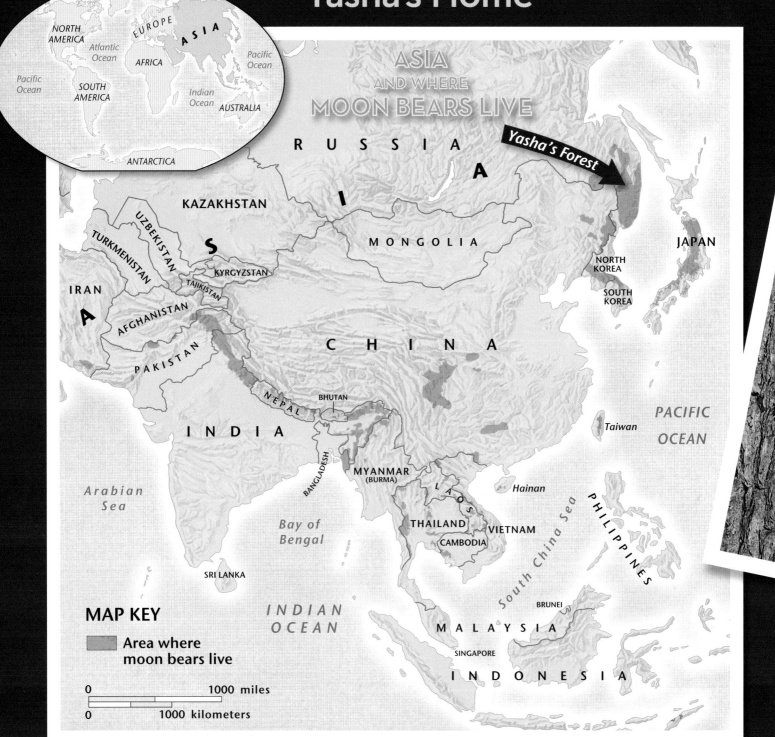

ASIA
AND WHERE
MOON BEARS LIVE

Inset map labels:
NORTH AMERICA
EUROPE
ASIA
Atlantic Ocean
AFRICA
Pacific Ocean
Pacific Ocean
SOUTH AMERICA
Indian Ocean
AUSTRALIA
ANTARCTICA

Main map labels:
RUSSIA
A S I A
Yasha's Forest
KAZAKHSTAN
MONGOLIA
JAPAN
NORTH KOREA
SOUTH KOREA
UZBEKISTAN
TURKMENISTAN
KYRGYZSTAN
TAJIKISTAN
IRAN
A
AFGHANISTAN
CHINA
PAKISTAN
NEPAL
BHUTAN
INDIA
Taiwan
PACIFIC OCEAN
BANGLADESH
MYANMAR (BURMA)
Arabian Sea
Bay of Bengal
Hainan
LAOS
THAILAND
VIETNAM
CAMBODIA
PHILIPPINES
South China Sea
SRI LANKA
INDIAN OCEAN
BRUNEI
MALAYSIA
SINGAPORE
INDONESIA

MAP KEY

Area where moon bears live

| 0 | 1000 miles |
| 0 | 1000 kilometers |

Yasha's crescent moon marking

All about Yasha and moon bears

- Moon bears come from Asia. Yasha, Shum, and Shiksha come from the mountains in the Russian Far East.

- Moon bears have beautiful black coats with a stripe on their chest that looks like the crescent moon in the sky.

- Moon bears are also called Asiatic black bears.

- These bears love trees. Moon bears create big nests in tree branches, where they go to eat, rest, hide, and even play.

- A moon bear weighs less than a pound when it is born but can weigh more than 400 pounds when grown!

- Liya and Sergey walked through the woods with Yasha and the other cubs 6 to 8 hours every day. They spent 2,000 hours observing the cubs for their study!

A note from the scientist

Asiatic black bears, known as moon bears (or *gimalajskij medved* in Russian), face numerous threats. In Russia and in parts of Asia, poaching and human expansion have had an impact on these gentle bears' way of life. It is estimated that the moon bear population has dropped by half in the last 30 years. Unfortunately, scientists don't know much about these secretive and rarely seen animals. In order to save this species from extinction, we need to better understand them. For this reason, my colleague Sergey Kolchin and I embarked on an amazing journey, living deep in the Durminskoe Game Preserve in Russia with little contact from the outside world for almost two years.

Yasha, Shum, and Shiksha were taken from the forest and brought to a nearby town where poachers most likely intended to sell them for a profit. My colleague and I managed to get each of them a few days later. Waiting for them was a bit like expecting a child. I was excited, but also nervous. I knew we had an important job to do and that the bears' ability to rejoin the wild rested with us.

Moon bear cubs are very cute and sometimes act much like humans. During our two-year study, I felt a great deal of affection and love toward them—and still do to this day— almost as though they were my own children. Providing a safe environment while remaining silent and detached from them was a difficult task. It was amazing and rewarding to watch these young cubs grow and learn to become adults, even if I couldn't show them every emotion I felt.

When Yasha was finally released into the wild at the end of August 2010, my feelings were mixed. He was ready to live on his own, and it was amazing to see his transformation into adulthood. We'd also collected invaluable data about moon bears' lives and habits, which is crucial to their conservation. But I also knew I'd never see Yasha or his adopted brother and sister again, so it was a little bittersweet. I am happy to report that the cubs have been spotted by remote camera traps several times, alive and well, and this news makes me very happy indeed.

I'd like to thank Dr. Valentin Pazhetnov, a zoologist who pioneered the methods that inspired our work. Also, I would like to thank the National Geographic Society and the Alertis Fund for Bear and Nature Conservation for their support of the project.

—Liya Pokrovskaya,
*National Geographic
Young Explorer*

Want to learn more about bears?

To see a video about moon bears featuring this project and Yasha, Shum, and Shiksha, visit news.national geographic.com/news/2010/05/ 100525-russia-moon-bears-video.

If you'd like to learn more about the orphaned bear cub project, Yasha's life after release, or any of Liya and Sergey's publications about the project, please email Liya at alopex@mail.ru.

WEBSITES

www.animalsasia.org
Conservation site dedicated to Asian animals, where you can sponsor a moon bear

www.bearbiology.com/index .php?id=36
Information on Asiatic black bears from the International Association for Bear Research and Management

http://beartrust.org
Site for Bear Trust International, an organization dedicated to bear conservation and school education projects

www.clean-forest.ru
The project website of Valentin Pazhetnov, Liya's mentor and orphaned bear cub rehabilitation pioneer (a Russian-language site that can be translated into English)

www.iucnredlist.org/apps/redlist/ details/22824/0
Page from the IUCN Red List of Threatened Species on moon bears

http://nationalzoo.si.edu/ Publications/ZooGoer/1999/2/ fact-asiaticblack.cfm
Fact sheet on Asiatic black bears from the Smithsonian National Zoological Park

BOOKS

Baines, Becky. *A Den Is a Bed for a Bear.* National Geographic Society, 2008.

Brown, Gary. *The Bear Almanac: A Comprehensive Guide to the Bears of the World,* 2nd ed. Lyons Press, 2009.

Craighead, Lance. *Bears of the World.* Voyageur Press, 2003.

Kilham, Benjamin, and Ed Gray. *Among the Bears: Raising Orphan Cubs in the Wild.* Henry Holt and Company, 2002.

Sartore, Joel. *Face to Face With Grizzlies.* National Geographic Society, 2007.

Schreiber, Anne. *Pandas.* National Geographic Society, 2010.

PLACES TO SEE MOON BEARS

In the United States
Denver Zoo, 2300 Steele Street, Denver, Colo.

Lincoln Park Zoo, 1215 N. 8th Street, Manitowoc, Wis.

Philadelphia Zoo, 3400 West Girard Avenue, Philadelphia, Pa.

Roger Williams Zoo, 1000 Elmwood Avenue, Providence, R.I.

Outside the United States
Animals Asia Foundation's Moon Bear Rescue Center, Chengdu, People's Republic of China

Asa Zoological Park, Hiroshima, Japan

Asiatic Black Bear Sanctuary, Luang Prabang, Laos

Balkasar Bear Sanctuary, Islamabad, Pakistan

International Fund for Animal Welfare's Panyu Bear Sanctuary, Guangdong, People's Republic of China

Kedarnath Wildlife Sanctuary, Uttarakhand, India

Moscow Zoo, Moscow, Russia

To Dr. Valentin Pazhetnov, our master, research adviser, and dear friend, who inspired us to save orphaned bears and gifted us his broad experience and skills in bear rehabilitation —Liya Pokrovskaya

For Kevin, my best friend and critic, and Violet, my own "cub." And special thanks to Clif Wiens for pointing the way, and Karine Aigner for making it happen —Lia Kvatum

Text copyright © 2012 Lia Kvatum
Photographs copyright © 2012 Liya Pokrovskaya unless otherwise noted
Compilation copyright © 2012 National Geographic Society

This project was funded in part by a National Geographic Society Young Explorer Grant.

Published by the National Geographic Society
John M. Fahey, Jr., *Chairman of the Board and Chief Executive Officer*
Timothy T. Kelly, *President*
Declan Moore, *Executive Vice President; President, Publishing*
Melina Gerosa Bellows, *Executive Vice President; Chief Creative Officer, Books, Kids, and Family*

Prepared by the Book Division
Hector Sierra, *Senior Vice President and General Manager*

Nancy Laties Feresten, *Senior Vice President, Editor in Chief, Children's Books*
Jonathan Halling, *Design Director, Books and Children's Publishing*
Jay Sumner, *Director of Photography, Children's Publishing*
Jennifer Emmett, *Editorial Director, Children's Books*
Eva Absher-Schantz, *Managing Art Director, Children's Books*
Carl Mehler, *Director of Maps*
R. Gary Colbert, *Production Director*
Jennifer A. Thornton, *Director of Managing Editorial*

Staff for This Book
Kate Olesin, *Project Editor*
Jay Sumner, *Illustrations Editor*
David M. Seager, *Art Director*
Grace Hill, *Associate Managing Editor*
Joan Gossett, *Production Editor*
Lewis R. Bassford, *Production Manager*
Susan Borke, *Legal and Business Affairs*
Kathryn Robbins, *Design Production Assistant*
Hillary Moloney, *Illustrations Assistant*

Manufacturing and Quality Management
Christopher A. Liedel, *Chief Financial Officer*
Phillip L. Schlosser, *Senior Vice President*
Chris Brown, *Technical Director*
Nicole Elliott, *Manager*
Rachel Faulise, *Manager*
Robert L. Barr, *Manager*

Photo Credits
Half-title page (Yasha walking), Sergey Kolchin; Title page, @mauritius images GmbH/Alamy; Yasha walking, Sergey Kolchin; Liya walking with Yasha, Sergey Kolchin; two bears playing in the water, Sergey Kolchin; Liya sitting in woods writing with bear nearby, Sergey Kolchin; landscape image, © Konstantin Mikhailov/Nature Picture Library; bear up a tree, Sergey Kolchin; tiger climbing tree, Marc Moritsch (Via Maurice Horndocker)/National Geographic Stock; map, Carl Mehler, Director of Maps, National Geographic Maps; bear in branches of tree looking at camera, Sergey Kolchin.

For more information, please call 1-800-NGS LINE (647-5463) or write to the following address:
National Geographic Society
1145 17th Street N.W.
Washington, D.C. 20036-4688 U.S.A.

Visit us online at nationalgeographic.com/books

For librarians and teachers:
ngchildrensbooks.org

More for kids from National Geographic:
kids.nationalgeographic.com

For information about special discounts for bulk purchases, please contact National Geographic Books Special Sales: ngspecsales@ngs.org

For rights or permissions inquiries, please contact National Geographic Books Subsidiary Rights: ngbookrights@ngs.org

Trade ISBN: 978-1-4263-1051-5
Reinforced library edition
ISBN: 978-1-4263-1076-8

Printed in Hong Kong
12/THK/1